CASTAWAY

SARAH STOCKTON

GLASS LYRE PRESS

Copyright © 2022 Sarah Stockton
Paperback ISBN: 978-1-941783-92-4

All rights reserved: Except for the purpose of quoting brief passages for review, no part of this book may be reproduced or transmitted in any form or by any means, electronic or mechanical, including photocopying, recording, or by any information storage and retrieval system, without permission in writing from the publisher.

Design & Layout: Steven Asmussen
Cover Art: Sarah Stockton
Author Photo: Andy Stockton

Glass Lyre Press, LLC
P.O. Box 2693
Glenview, IL 60025
www.GlassLyrePress.com

CASTAWAY

For Andy
my lighthouse, my anchor, my love

CONTENTS

The Sailor's Daughter	1
Seawalls Protect	2
Take Comfort, or Is It Cover	3
Haven	4
Summer is Forever Away	5
Atlantis	6
Sleeping	7
Warning Signs	9
Castaway	10
In Which I Attempt Metaphors in Conversation with my Doctor	11
I Hunger for Your Touch	15
The Binding	16
Myliobatis Californica	17
Salt and Other Spells	18
What I Have Done, and What I Have Failed to Do	19
From the Diaries: Dawn	20
From the Diaries: Noon	21
From the Diaries: Dusk	22
Home	23
Acknowledgements	25
About the Author	27

The Sailor's Daughter

My father has become a small boy demanding attention, tacking
across the lanes in search of whatever he forgot. Chasing dreams
of blue and yellow boats, adrift in the forgotten harbors of his mind.

I stay vigilant, my own life tethered to his, waiting my turn
at the tiller. A sea chest filled with trash and treasure trailing
in my father's wake as he greets every stranger like a long-lost love.

He asks me for a star chart to navigate by— the ley lines marked
for home just in case he gets lost. We will set sail as soon as the sky
clears and the wind lifts I say, raising my glass. Anchors aweigh.

Seawalls Protect

the stubborn drive of our damaged lives,
even as the foundations
start to crack. Someone who can't
think straight will continue to try, stabbing words
like pinned butterflies until the colors run out.

I've been you, counting out change for groceries
and then having to put something back.
And yet, we decide not to quit but to keep on–
we line up our various devices like
tiny battlements, surrounded by grief-filled moats.

While I'm not long for this world
I still admire its contenders—
waiting in line for the food they can barely
eat, *so freaking hot,* vision blurred by sweat,
one step from homeless. One step off.

May I not retreat today from the agreement
we've all made to see it through. I love
everyone who tries one more time, checks
how they look before they go out, constructs
safe shelters as the seawalls around them give way.

Take Comfort, or Is It Cover

in the knowledge that certain people
who once did you harm are gone

in knowing
joy abides in the body like an octopus
goddess cavorting in her sea-spursed den

multiplying arms, Salome veils swooning
in memories of the body's delight

crossing the currents of despair and back
nimbly balanced between now and before
all within the same thought

Haven

She takes a little blue pill on Wednesdays
and Saturdays—gray on the rest. Today
in the Northwest, signs of blue are disappearing

into the smoke and clouds of winter.
Even the Steller's Jays have abandoned
these woods, leaving crows, barred owls

and juncos to chatter among the last
of the berries on the blue spectrum, sweet
summer jewels in shades of dying.

When she swallows a little blue pill on Wednesdays
 and Saturdays, her bed is less inviting.
We walk by the Salish shore

scavenging for mussel shells, seabird tracks,
bits of glass. Restored, she feels like that jay
extending her beak toward winter

preparing a hermitage out of discarded
feathers and frayed prayer flag strips,
ink fading into unknowable requests.

Summer is Forever Away

I've travelled beyond normalcy's curtain
lying on the bed of my own inconsequence

it's quiet here, window glass cold

someone kind promises summer, sings
tales of exchanging fish scales for bare skin

dead tree branches for kelp tresses
bursting from barnacle's grip, floating
toward a horizon which is forever

away   I should be ready by then

wrapped in golden sails
as sorrow slips past the fact-checkers

and despondence cuts her winter hair

Atlantis

When you found me
                in that final, sundown hour
I was already far beyond the swell
                tide ~ innocence receding

craving the sandy curve
                of my hip, my webbed
and banished soul, you caught
                me after I had descended

into poverty, into loneliness
                two scavengers, you
reached to taste the sun
                between my shoulder blades

my shell-encrusted breasts
                ~ jellyfish burns
on my inner thighs ~ salt water
                trickling with regret

SLEEPING   *(WITH A PHRASE FROM MARY OLIVER)*

at the bus stop, on the front porch, sticky kitchen floor

on a couch/ mother's

couch/stranger's

couch/ abandoned

Sleeping

In a tent, truck-bed, border, cell

a classroom, library, church pew, desk

diner booth, B&B, youth hostel

guestroom, haybarn, hospital

Sleeping

under a tree, on the shore, pool float, boat

backseat of the car/van/limousine/bus

in a seven-story carpark, on an airplane, airport hotel

motel lobby, motel balcony, motel floor

      backside

           right side

left side

      belly

      wrapped in the *soft animal body*

Warning Signs *(a variation of the Japanese Zhihitsu)*

A friend writes in calligraphy *blessings of cedar/* My handwriting is illegible/ I record the signs in secret, readable by no one/

Pagans say *first, do no harm/* The tarot card I pulled this morning was reversed; The Hanged One, upright, is already upside down

making it hard to read, the meaning obscure/ Blessings are nowhere, or all around/ I find a car-crushed newt on the road, beside a fallen

paper wasps' nest constructed of tiny, abandoned hexagons/ I place these tangible signatures of death on a cedar stump, a roadside shrine/

I'm not above sending blessings to the car which killed the newt, forgiving the unintentional harm/ The Death card is followed by Temperance, card

of balance, of writing things down/ If life is a lemniscate, then what is unknowable is never truly dead/ I take three ferries to reach my friend/

At the last boat crossing, I abandon my car and walk on/ We will read the signs under her cedar tree/ I believe in no accidents/ I believe in the upside down/

Castaway

a broken, overturned boat
on a stormy day

abandoned in long reeds
on an empty shore

someone living beneath

In Which I Attempt Metaphors in Conversation with my Doctor

~ My heart is at the center
             of a hybrid ecosystem. Consider
a tree
             in which blood-sap ferries
the biotics
             of essential energy

    ~ I am the ghost rider
        of a virus that will live
longer
        than my own beliefs
and which eviscerates
        everything

~ this fragile body
    is floating on blood-borne waters
    and I'm sinking

~ If the heart is
        the center of the trunk of a tree
then my body
        is a carved and weathered cedar boat
rocking in the wind's wake
        rocking
                I rock myself to sleep

I Hunger for Your Touch
(by way of the Righteous Brothers)

In school, I might have done better
in math if we had drawn the triangle
of the soul, located the hypotenuse

of the holy body and discussed whether
love could be transmuted or disappear
into infinity because some days I walk

across the pacific tidepools and by a glance
of fractal light I see you, even while knowing
 you're trapped in an unchained mind.

I want to fly across the country
just to feel your touch, to breathe your breath
regardless of the dangerous symmetry

Are you still mine?

The Binding

we exchange dreams
yours about a manta ray and underwater caves
mine about nothing

    I can admit out loud

we advise each other to meditate
to drink less, or more

    we forgive each other

nothing has been the same
since the day we anchored
in the perilous harbor, anticipating

    the precipice of the last horizon—

there is no answer
when we ask each other
how much time is enough

Myliobatis Californica

<pre>
                         sea bat,
                       all I have left
                  is the memory of your shadow.
              I was a small creature in the context
           of the deep, more plankton than mammal, not as pretty
         as a mermaid, swimming to escape. Punga, the Maori *atua*, took
  me under his wing, the one known as manta, a sister to *Hahalua*, who would not
          sting as it glided over me in the teal Catalina sea. I had a true way
               of knowing then, swimming with creatures of the pelagic
                   unafraid of the great diamond, the geometry
                      of four: self, ocean, salt, and the holy
                            creatures sailors called
                                   dragons
                                 black
                                              salt
                          wings
                                      undul

                                ating
</pre>

Salt and Other Spells

We were water once
cyclical, transforming
salt and sediment into scales
anadromous/

moving from sea into sweet water
catadromous/
fresh to salt
to spawn/ traveling

in deep sea channels
transitioning/
from silvery blue
to darker, going home

as we, floundering at water's edge
turn in four directions/
three visions/ seven cycles
scrying into water

What I Have Done, and What I Have Failed to Do

A young man collapsed inside himself, jittery, hoodie pulled down, body
folded into the corner of the pew like a broken beach chair

abandoned in the shallows. It came to me then *I will never be more than I am right now*
so I sat down next to him, smiling at the elderly women around us, carefully

keeping my hands where he could see them, fingers open in my lap, steady breathing
ready to receive a whispered confession but annoyed at the way he scrounged

 in the plastic bag beneath his feet. I was afraid of his cat's eye marble stare, the bloody
medical tape wrapped too tight around his knuckles and hands, pain swelling

the bruised and burning flesh he pressed to my flesh as we passed the peace.
Let me help you with your suffering, my son, is what I didn't say. Where I live

blue herons stand about in still water, fly across the uncluttered sky.
I am always glad to witness their grace, their flight, before I turn away.

From the Diaries: Dawn

Dear Anais-
Remember exchanging those lists of past lovers?
I left a few names out- revisions forthcoming.
Did you like that photo I posted of my mother?
I look like her right now, no filter. I wish
you were here, wrapped in your silk shawl
like a dragonfly in the dawn.

From the Diaries: Noon

Dear Anais-
I am taking your advice and leaving this place.
We were up all night, dancing wild until
I fell overboard in disgrace. The houseboat leaks
but your diaries are still safe. I'm banned
from the docks until I pay the rent.
I guess I should have lead with that.

From the Diaries: Dusk

Dear Anais-
Do you think it's time for me to go?
An old man is throwing fish heads at the gulls, dead eyes
glassy and spinning now toward heaven, now the sea.
The harbormaster looks away when I pass him
on the dock. Please come back, write me into your story.
The sky is lowering; the houseboat, sinking into the deep.

Home *(A VARIATION ON THE GHAZAL)*

I will take the first exit, the last ferry, a sinking boat or wild horse,
the backseat of a stranger's car; any means necessary to reach home.

Cockroaches and rats become roommates. Landlords evict, mortgages
dig their own graves, trailers burn down. Still, there's no place like home.

Not every family offers a place to belong. 12-Step meetings, libraries, even
a crowded food court in a shopping mall can mimic the solace of home.

These days I live in a landlocked house, grieving for people alone, those trapped
at the border or hiding in the woods— sleeping under a tree they call home.

You said *beloved, you were born here,* this is home; but I say that without you
no real estate, landscape, or country could ever be my home.

Acknowledgements

"Haven" was published by *About Place Journal*, Summer 2021
"What I Have Done and What I Have Failed to Do" was published by
    Glass Poetry, June 2019
"Salt and Other Spells" was published by *Luna Luna Magazine*,
    November 2019
"From the Diaries" was published by *The Shallow Ends*, January 2019

With special thanks to my fellow members of the workshop taught by the poet Elizabeth Bradfield, via Orion Magazine, where many of the poems collected here were first drafted.

About the Author

Sarah Stockton, MA is the Editor-in-Chief of River Mouth Review and the author of Time's Apprentice (dancing girl press, 2021). Individual poems can be found in *About Place Journal, EcoTheo Review, Glass Journal, Crab Creek Review,* and *Psaltery & Lyre,* to name a few. A freelance editor and writer, Sarah is also the author of two books on spirituality, a trained spiritual director and creativity mentor, and taught at the University of San Francisco for several years. Sarah makes her current home in the Pacific Northwest, by the Salish Sea. www.sarahstockton.com

Sarah Stockton, MA is the Editor-in-Chief of River Mouth Review and the author of Time's Apprentice (dancing girl press, 2021). Individual poems can be found in *About Place Journal, EcoTheo Review, Glass Journal, Crab Creek Review*, and *Psaltery & Lyre*, to name a few. A freelance editor and writer, Sarah is also the author of two books on spirituality, a trained spiritual director and creativity mentor, and taught at the University of San Francisco for several years. "Sarah" makes her current home in the Pacific Northwest, by the Salish Sea. www.sarahstockton.com

Glass Lyre Press

exceptional works to replenish the spirit

Glass Lyre Press is an independent literary publisher interested in technically accomplished, stylistically distinct, and original work. Glass Lyre seeks diverse writers that possess a dynamic aesthetic and an ability to emotionally and intellectually engage a wide audience of readers.

Glass Lyre's vision is to connect the world through language and art. We hope to expand the scope of poetry and short fiction for the general reader through exceptionally well-written books, which evoke emotion, provide insight, and resonate with the human spirit.

Poetry Collections
Poetry Chapbooks
Select Short & Flash Fiction
Anthologies

www.GlassLyrePress.com

www.ingramcontent.com/pod-product-compliance
Lightning Source LLC
Chambersburg PA
CBHW030203100526
44592CB00009B/415